ISO 22301:2019

An introduction to a business continuity
management system (BCMS)

ISO 22301:2019

An introduction to a business continuity
management system (BCMS)

ALAN CALDER

IT Governance Publishing

Every possible effort has been made to ensure that the information contained in this book is accurate at the time of going to press, and the publisher and the author cannot accept responsibility for any errors or omissions, however caused. Any opinions expressed in this book are those of the author, not the publisher. Websites identified are for reference only, not endorsement, and any website visits are at the reader's own risk. No responsibility for loss or damage occasioned to any person acting, or refraining from action, as a result of the material in this publication can be accepted by the publisher or the author.

Apart from any fair dealing for the purposes of research or private study, or criticism or review, as permitted under the Copyright, Designs and Patents Act 1988, this publication may only be reproduced, stored or transmitted, in any form, or by any means, with the prior permission in writing of the publisher or, in the case of reprographic reproduction, in accordance with the terms of licences issued by the Copyright Licensing Agency. Enquiries concerning reproduction outside those terms should be sent to the publisher at the following address:

IT Governance Publishing Ltd
Unit 3, Clive Court
Bartholomew's Walk
Cambridgeshire Business Park
Ely, Cambridgeshire
CB7 4EA
United Kingdom
www.itgovernancepublishing.co.uk

© Alan Calder 2020

Formerly published as _ISO23301 – A Pocket Guide_ in the United Kingdom in 2013 by IT Governance Publishing.

First edition published in the United Kingdom in 2020 by IT Governance Publishing

ISBN 978-1-78778-227-3

CONTENTS

INTRODUCTION

In an increasingly volatile world, exemplified by the 2020 COVID-19 pandemic, organisations are looking at business continuity with new eyes. While most organisations believe they are prepared for disruptive incidents, the events of 2020 have proved otherwise. The need for business continuity has never been clearer.

This pocket guide is intended to provide the reader with an understanding of the basics of business continuity and ISO 22301:2019, the international standard that describes the specification for a business continuity management system (BCMS). It is not an implementation guide.

Like many management systems, ISO 22301 is supported by an 'explanatory' standard. ISO 22313:2020 contains detailed explanations of and useful guidance on the parts of ISO 22301 and their implementation.[1] Anyone implementing an ISO 22301-compliant BCMS should strongly consider purchasing ISO 22313 in addition to this book.

---

[1] ISO 22313:2020 *Security and resilience – Business continuity management systems – Guidance on the use of ISO 22301.*

CHAPTER 1: WHAT IS BUSINESS CONTINUITY?

In any organisational endeavour, be it a business, public body or not-for-profit organisation, a key factor of success is that it can operate without being interrupted by unforeseen factors. To do this, organisations develop contingencies to ensure that resources and productivity are not disrupted by everyday events.

Everyday events are one thing – significant disruptive incidents are quite another. Most contingencies are developed on an intuitive basis and are intended to deal with short-term problems; when the problems are longer term, or of a scale or nature not anticipated by the designer, they often fall short of what is needed to ensure continued operation, putting the organisation at risk.

Business continuity management is a systematic process of risk management and planning designed to ensure that an organisation can quickly return to an acceptable level of service after a disruptive incident.

Why does business continuity matter?

Many people regard business continuity as a form of risk management or insurance; a means of ensuring that, if something goes wrong, there is a way of limiting or even eliminating the impact.

However, there are other important reasons, outlined below, why organisations should have a business continuity management programme.

Licence to operate

Most businesses are allowed to do what they do provided they operate within the law. However, many public bodies and an increasing number of businesses (for example, in the financial sector) operate under some form of licence, permission or authority that could, under certain circumstances, be withdrawn.

For many, this can be considered an operational risk, and a risk to operations is a risk to the organisation's ability to continue to function. Critically, each organisation must decide, as a matter of policy, whether risks associated with its licence to operate should be included within the scope of its BCMS (policy and scope are described in more detail in chapter 4).

Competitive edge

As the risk of suppliers falling victim to operational issues becomes more visible, many organisations are seeking formal assurance that their suppliers will be able to continue supplying them in the event of a disruptive incident. Operational resilience is a common requirement in supplier due diligence processes (alongside other criteria including financial stability, quality management systems and information security), yet many organisations still treat it as an afterthought.

The existence of a recognised business continuity standard provides a real benchmark against which organisations can satisfy themselves as to their suppliers' operational resilience. For suppliers, this means that having a BCMS that complies with – or, better still, is certified to – ISO 22301 can amount to a significant competitive advantage.

Insurance

Many organisations have business interruption cover as part of their business insurance portfolio. This cover will usually compensate the organisation for loss of profit in the event of an interruption for a period called the 'indemnity period', which can range from just a few months up to one or two years.

Unfortunately, interruption cover does not compensate for any loss outside of the indemnity period, rarely includes major events such as terrorism or pandemic threats as a matter of course (at least, not without paying an additional premium), and does not compensate for the loss of future business that so frequently follows a major disruption. Even if you are compensated for the earnings lost during the disruption, the customers you lose are unlikely to return.

While useful, business interruption cover usually comes at a significant cost to the organisation, and rarely offers much protection against a truly serious disruption. While insurance remains an important component of any organisation's resilience in the face of operational risks and interruptions, it should always be seen as complementary to business continuity management (BCM), not as a substitute. The existence of a BCMS, however, often provides an opportunity to reduce the amount of cover that is needed and, therefore, the insurance premium.

Corporate governance

Corporate governance is frequently referred to as a reason for 'doing' business continuity, but often without a proper explanation of its significance.

The *UK Corporate Governance Code 2018* includes a requirement to "monitor the company's risk management and internal control systems and, at least annually, carry out a review of their effectiveness and report on that review in the annual report".[2]

The *Guidance on Risk Management, Internal Control and Related Financial and Business Reporting* (which provides specific guidance on compliance with the *Corporate Governance Code*), while focusing significantly on financial controls, is clear that the organisation must ensure it is

---

[2] Financial Reporting Council, *The UK Corporate Governance Code 2018*, July 2018, *www.frc.org.uk/directors/corporate-governance-and-stewardship/uk-corporate-governance-code*, section 29.

able to "respond appropriately to risks and significant control failures and to safeguard its assets".[3]

While neither the letter of the *Corporate Governance Code* nor the *Guidance* state that listed companies or those seeking listing must have a business continuity plan (BCP), the spirit of 'responding appropriately' in today's business climate is usually taken to mean that business continuity planning is a component of the organisation's operational risk management and internal control measures.

For privately owned companies and those limited by guarantee, stakeholders expect that boards will also respond appropriately to operational risks, just as they do to financial and legislative ones, and that appropriate business continuity arrangements will be in place.

The best way to provide evidence of appropriate management and control of the operational risks that could lead to business interruption is to develop and implement a BCMS that meets the requirements of ISO 22301 and is, preferably, also externally certified against the Standard.

---

[3] Financial Reporting Council, *Guidance on Risk Management, Internal Control and Related Financial and Business Reporting*, September 2014, *www.frc.org.uk/directors/corporate-governance-and-stewardship/uk-corporate-governance-code/frc-guidance-for-boards-and-board-committees*, section 4.

CHAPTER 2: TERMS AND DEFINITIONS

The following definitions are taken from ISO 22301:2019. A number of the definitions are supplemented by notes, and the reader should turn to a copy of the Standard for further information.

Audit – systematic, independent and documented process for obtaining audit evidence and evaluating it objectively to determine the extent to which the audit criteria are fulfilled.

Business continuity – capability of the organisation to continue delivery of products or services at acceptable time frames at a predefined capacity during a disruption.

Business continuity plan (BCP) – documented information that guides an organisation to respond to a disruption and resume, recover, and restore the delivery of products and services consistent with its business continuity objectives.

Business impact analysis (BIA) – process of analysing activities and the effect that a business disruption might have upon them.

Corrective action – action to eliminate the cause(s) of a nonconformity and to prevent recurrence.

Disruption – incident, whether anticipated or unanticipated, that causes an unplanned, negative deviation from the expected delivery of products and services according to an organisation's objectives.

Incident – event that can be, or could lead to, a disruption, loss, emergency or crisis.

Interested party – person or organisation that can affect, be affected by, or perceive itself to be affected by a decision or activity.

Management system – set of interrelated or interacting elements of an organisation to establish policies and objectives, and processes to achieve those objectives.

Nonconformity – non-fulfilment of a requirement [of ISO 22301].

Resource – all assets (including plant and equipment), people, skills, information, technology, premises, and supplies and information (whether electronic or not) that an organisation has to have available to use, when needed, in order to operate and meet its objective.

Risk – effect of uncertainty on objectives.

CHAPTER 3: A BRIEF HISTORY OF BUSINESS CONTINUITY MANAGEMENT

The genesis of BCM as a formal discipline arguably lies in the introduction of computers to business. The considerable benefits derived from the use of computers in speeding up business processes and improving productivity soon became dulled by the realisation that computers were likely to go wrong and that, when they did, this tended to have a significant impact.

So 'disaster recovery' appeared: services provided initially by computer manufacturers and later by dedicated service providers to help organisations restore their computer systems in the event of failure.

Over time, disaster recovery evolved from a solely technological consideration to one encompassing the entire organisation, culminating in the publication of early business continuity standards such as PAS 56: 2003 *Guide to business continuity management*. The arrival of BS 25999-1 in 2006 and BS 25999-2 in 2007 defined a formal approach for UK organisations engaged in anything to do with business continuity or resilience, and the possibility of national accreditation for those looking to set themselves apart from their competitors.

As worldwide demand for a business continuity standard grew, the International Organization for Standardization (ISO) developed a new business continuity standard, which was published in 2012.

ISO 22301:2012 *Societal security – Business continuity management systems – Requirements* described the specification for a BCMS – a formal methodology that organisations could use to prepare for and respond effectively to disruptive events.

As an ISO standard, ISO 22301 offered benefits over the older standards. It was developed to match the movement towards a common structure for management system standards, allowing it to integrate easily with other management systems and streamlining adoption by experienced management system practitioners. It also offered the opportunity to achieve internationally recognised certification – a valuable mark of assurance in an increasingly insecure age and a significant advance over the limited national accreditation available for BS 25999.

October 2019 saw the release of ISO 22301:2019 *Security and resilience — Business continuity management systems — Requirements*. While largely an administrative revision, the new standard retains all the benefits of the 2012 edition, but uses clearer language and clarifies several key concepts, making the process of implementing a BCMS easier and more accessible.

CHAPTER 4: THE BUSINESS CONTINUITY MANAGEMENT SYSTEM

Ultimately, the key deliverable of business continuity planning is a BCP that works. Every organisation should satisfy itself that its BCP is fit for purpose, otherwise the investment in developing the plan will be wasted.

The BCMS consists of a set of requirements designed to ensure that the plan is, indeed, fit for purpose. It does this by:

- Understanding and analysing the business recovery requirements so that the impact of an incident or interruption is properly understood and balanced across the organisation;
- Identifying the resources the organisation needs in order to withstand the worst possible situation and ensuring that they will be available;
- Creating a documented plan that is based upon valid assumptions, delivers the required recovery outcomes and is properly understood, or 'owned', by those that are likely to use it; and
- Testing the plan, resources and people involved so that everything remains up to date, capabilities are adequate and the best level of assurance can be given as to the effectiveness of the plan.

These four key components will be well understood by anyone involved in running an organisation. However, the biggest weakness of business continuity planning is that the plan itself may never be needed. BCM is a contingent discipline and not 'core business' to any organisation except those involved in providing BCM products and services. Because of this, many plans do not get the long-term attention necessary to ensure they are reliable and effective at the point of need.

A comprehensive BCMS goes further than the functional components listed above. It includes policy, commitment and engagement from top management, creating the 'ownership' throughout the organisation that ensures the plans and arrangements are adequately maintained and can be put into practice.

Perhaps the most fundamental principle of the BCMS is that it is an iterative process, not a one-off exercise. ISO 22301 accounts for this through use of the Plan-Do-Check-Act (PDCA) methodology. As the name suggests, PDCA is a structured and iterative approach to continual improvement, and has been adopted across many management system standards due to its simplicity and ease of use.

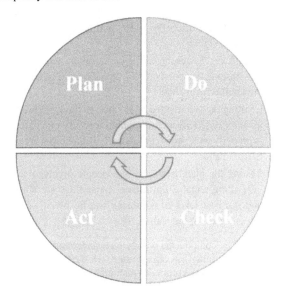

Figure 1: The PDCA cycle

CHAPTER 5: ISO 22301 – BCMS – REQUIREMENTS

Similar to other standards, ISO 22301 devotes its first three sections to:

1. Scope;
2. Normative references; and
3. Terms and definitions.

The remaining seven sections are summarised as follows:

4 Context of the organisation

This section of the Standard is concerned with identifying the key operational aspects of your organisation, such as:

- Understanding the context your organisation operates within;
- The needs and expectations of interested parties;
- Legal and regulatory requirements related to the continuity of the services or products you offer; and
- The scope of the management system.

The context referred to in the first point is that of the legal, regulatory, financial, commercial and other aspects – both internal and external – that affect the day-to-day operation of the organisation. 'Interested parties' might include employees, regulators, suppliers, shareholders, insurers, and so on. From both the context of the organisation and the requirements of interested parties, various risks and opportunities related to the BCMS will arise – these are treated in section 6 of the Standard.

It is important to note that the Standard expressly requires you to account for legal requirements that relate to the continuity of your services or products (in addition to non-continuity-related legal requirements that fall within the context of the organisation). If you operate essential services or offer digital services, for example, you may need to comply with the EU Directive on security of network and information systems (the NIS Directive; implemented by the NIS Regulations in the UK), which contains specific provisions on business continuity.

The scope of the management system refers to the boundaries and limits of the BCMS. Many organisations consider all their operations to be in scope, but depending on the products or services you offer, it may not be necessary to ensure continuity for all of them. In such cases, ensure that anything that is excluded from the scope is definitely something the organisation can 'live without' in the event of a disruption, and justify the exclusion in writing.

5 Leadership and commitment

This section of the Standard addresses:

- Leadership and commitment with respect to BCM;
- The business continuity policy; and
- Roles, responsibilities and authorities for the BCMS.

Leadership and commitment

Leadership and commitment to the BCMS is critical. BCM has evolved as a management discipline because it is the only way of comprehensively managing the risks of business interruption; if the board does not appreciate the gravity of the subject, the BCMS is unlikely to be very effective. The board must understand that hoping for the best, winging it or assuming that things will 'just happen' put the very future of the organisation at risk.

ISO 22301 requires the organisation's management to demonstrate commitment, and to be involved in the BCMS development process and in the ongoing review of its components. One of the best ways of making this commitment 'real' is to establish a business continuity committee or a risk management committee, with membership from all parts of the organisation. This committee should lead the development of the

BCMS, review its effectiveness and oversee its long-term maintenance.

Policy

The business continuity policy defines the organisation's overall approach – how and why it 'does' continuity. It should be concise and include statements setting out the board's commitment and intent to comply with the requirements of the Standard, applicable legal requirements, and so on. The policy should also provide a framework for setting BCMS objectives.

You should write your policy in plain language so that it can be understood by any interested party, particularly employees and customers. It should be in a format that can be easily communicated, and should be approved and reviewed regularly by the board.

Roles, responsibilities and authorities

Naturally, it is necessary to define appropriate roles and responsibilities to ensure the BCMS is implemented and adequately maintained. Large organisations might have a dedicated business continuity manager, while smaller ones often merge the role with an existing managerial position – for example, a quality manager.

Regardless of how the organisation assigns responsibility for the BCMS, someone must be responsible for making sure the BCMS adheres to the requirements of the Standard, and for reporting on the performance of the BCMS to top management.

It is important that this person understands management systems and has a genuine appreciation for the need for business continuity. Passing the responsibility to someone who doesn't understand what the BCMS requires, or fails to appreciate how important business continuity is, is a sure recipe for failure.

Implementing a BCMS should be approached as a formal project and supported by all that entails – resources, project management, budgets, etc.

6 Planning

Section 6 of the Standard discusses the following:

- The risks and opportunities to the BCMS that arise from the context of the organisation and the requirements of interested parties.
- Business continuity objectives and planning to achieve them.
- Planning changes to the BCMS.

The risks, opportunities and requirements that arise from the context of the organisation and interested parties must be addressed to ensure that the BCMS works and is not itself disrupted or impaired. Any changes to the BCMS, in turn, must be planned to ensure they do not have a detrimental effect on the BCMS or the BCP.

Perhaps the most important part of section 6 is the requirement to define objectives for the BCMS and plan the approach the organisation will take to achieve them. The objectives form the basis for continual improvement of the BCMS – for example, reducing your overall recovery time – and need to be monitored and reported on accordingly.

The Standard contains specific requirements for what objectives should look like. One method that meets those requirements is 'SMART' – objectives that are *specific*, *measurable*, *achievable*, *realistic* and *time-bound*.

7 Support

Section 7 of ISO 22301 describes requirements for supporting the BCMS, including:

- Resources;
- Competence and awareness programmes;
- A communications plan; and
- Document control.

Resources

Implementing and maintaining a BCMS inevitably requires resources. While implementation is naturally a front-loaded exercise, maintaining the BCMS over the long term is every bit as important. You will need to consider personnel, equipment and infrastructure, facilities, and more, depending on the nature of your business.

Competence and awareness

The Standard's requirements around competence are fairly straightforward – make sure you know what competence is needed for the BCMS project, then acquire it, whether through hiring new staff or training existing ones. It is important to keep appropriate records, both in respect of the competence you have determined is necessary, and how you set about acquiring it.

The awareness requirements are also reasonably straightforward, but their simplicity downplays their importance. Awareness is key to the success of BCM. Just as top management must make a real commitment, everyone else in the organisation must understand why business continuity is important and the role they play in making sure the BCP is effective.

In the event of an incident, many people in the organisation will be required to respond in one way or another, and the better their level of awareness of the plan and the part they play in it, the more likely it is that the plan will be effective.

For most employees, basic awareness training should be sufficient, but those employees with specific responsibilities in respect of the plan will likely require more detailed training. It can be useful to define those responsibilities in job descriptions and review them during performance reviews.

Communication

Another relatively straightforward requirement, this part of the Standard covers the communications related to the BCMS, whether internal or external. Internal communications might include notifying relevant employees of changes to the BCP, for example, while external communications might involve making the business continuity policy or other information available to stakeholders. How and when to communicate about your BCMS is, ultimately, up to the organisation, but you should retain a record of all key communications to inform and improve future exercises and responses.

Document control

Document control is a key component of all management systems, and a BCMS is no exception. Key documents like business impact analyses (BIAs) and, of course, the plan itself need to be controlled to ensure the latest version is used. The same is true for the procedures, work instructions, risk assessments and other processes that make up the core of the BCMS. Using an out-of-date document can have a range of negative consequences – if the way you assess risks changes, for example, but assessments continue to be performed using the old method, you may end up under- or over-estimating the risks that affect the BCP or the BCMS itself, and consequently implementing inappropriate or ineffective measures.

8 Operation

This part of the Standard is the core of ISO 22301 – the section that defines the processes and plans that make business continuity possible. As a result, it is the longest single section in the Standard. It contains:

- Operational planning and control;
- Business impact analysis and risk assessment;
- Business continuity strategies and solutions;
- Business continuity plans and procedures;
- Exercise programmes; and
- Evaluation of business continuity documentation and capabilities.

Operational planning and control

Section 6 of the Standard asks that you identify risks (and opportunities) that can affect the operation of the BCMS. It also asks you to implement planning and control processes to make sure those risks are managed, including risks that arise from any changes to the BCMS and risks that arise from outsourced processes and suppliers. You also need to document the processes enough for you to be confident that they have been carried out.

Business impact analysis

To develop a BCP, you first need to understand the impact that would occur if your activities are disrupted and how quickly each activity needs to be resumed. Achieving this in a systematic, repeatable manner is what BIA is all about.

The Standard describes the BIA process in a series of steps. While this pocket guide cannot explain it in detail, we can summarise the principles.[4]

The first thing to do is to identify your activities. Most organisations already segment their activities in one way or another – sales department, IT support, warranty and repair, etc. – so in most cases you can simply consider each department or business area in turn and identify the core output.

Once you have determined your activities, you can consider the impact on the organisation if each of them is interrupted. In the majority of cases, impact will increase the longer the disruption lasts, and your analysis must account for this. It is necessary to establish the length of interruption that each activity, and the organisation as a whole, can tolerate – the maximum tolerable period of disruption (MTPD).

---

[4] For more information, see IT Governance's complete list of BCM and ISO 22301 resources, *www.itgovernance.co.uk/shop/category/bcm-and-iso-22301*.

Once you have defined MTPDs for each activity, you can then determine how quickly you need each one to become operational (even if at reduced capacity) after a disruption. This is known as a recovery time objective (RTO). The RTO is the basis on which recovery activities are prioritised – the shorter the RTO, the higher the priority – and once you know which activities to resume first, you can then identify the resources required to do so, and account for any dependencies that the activity relies on.

Like the rest of BCM, BIA is a recurring activity. The frequency with which BIA reviews are conducted is up to your organisation, but they should always be conducted after any major change in how the organisation operates.

The first iteration of BIA will naturally be resource intensive, as it will be necessary to map all the activities the organisation performs. This phase is likely to take anywhere from a few weeks to a few months to achieve, depending on the size and complexity of the organisation.

Risk assessment

The counterpart to the BIA process is the need to identify possible disruptions. The Standard requires that you use a risk assessment process to identify the disruptions your organisation might face, and the potential risks each one poses. This feeds into the development of the business continuity plan – BIA provides the information on the key activities that must be recovered, and risk assessment defines the disruptions the continuity plan must guard against.

Risk assessment is a complex discipline, and the Standard points the reader to ISO 31000 for guidance.[5] Section 6.4 of ISO 31000 describes risk assessment methodology in broad terms and is useful for those unfamiliar with key principles; for those familiar with the principles but seeking more guidance on how they work in practice, ISO 31010 describes applied risk assessment

---

[5] ISO 31000: 2018 *Risk Management – Guidelines.*

techniques.[6] From a practical perspective, most organisations already operate a risk assessment process and it is likely that you can apply or adapt it to identify and assess likely disruptions.

Identification of potential disruptions is best achieved by a scenario-based approach (fire in the server room, flooding in the main production area, etc). For each scenario, determine the risk of the scenario coming to pass and its potential outcome: for example, a fire in the server room will not only damage or destroy computer hardware, but may also affect the structural integrity of the building, or disturb in-situ asbestos.

This process should produce a range of scenarios considered likely enough and disruptive enough to be worth planning for in the BCP. Self-evidently impossible scenarios can be excluded, but take care not to confuse the impossible with the highly improbable. There is no sense expending resources to plan for a volcanic eruption if your organisation operates from a single site in London, but a global pandemic – which, until 2020, most would have considered extremely unlikely – is something all organisations are vulnerable to.

Business continuity strategies and solutions

With the data from your BIA and your risk assessments, you can determine your business continuity strategies and solutions. This is a complex area that feeds directly into your BCP, but the Standard only provides a basic outline of the process.

It is first necessary to differentiate between strategies and solutions. Strategies are the long-term plans that you employ to meet your business continuity goals; solutions are the means by which you implement those strategies and achieve those goals. A recovery strategy for a data centre losing power, for example, might involve regular backups, uninterruptible power supplies (UPSs), and alternative server and storage hardware in a different region – three solutions that each deal with a different aspect of the disruption and are employed at different times.

---

[6] ISO 31010: 2019 *Risk management – Risk assessment techniques.*

Strategies should consider solutions that are applied before, during and after a disruptive incident to be truly effective – after all, our data centre recovery strategy would not be very effective without backups taken before the incident occurs. The UPS solution also needs to be implemented beforehand but is only likely to be used during an incident and will only mitigate the power outage for a relatively short period of time. The alternative server and storage hardware in another region would be used if the power outage continues for long enough that the UPS can no longer sustain the operation of the data centre.

Ultimately, it is up to the organisation to identify, select and implement strategies and solutions, and to provide the resources those solutions rely on. If one solution can be used in multiple strategies, so much the better, but take care to ensure adequate capacity in such cases to avoid conflicts when developing your continuity plan.

Business continuity plans and procedures

As the core component of the BCMS, the BCP uses all the information determined in the earlier sections of the Standard. However, the plan is not merely a single document – it comprises several parts, all of which work together to ensure the organisation recovers effectively.

What the business continuity plan includes

Procedures

The plan must be backed up by procedures that detail the actions necessary for recovery. The Standard describes requirements for those procedures, including one that is often neglected: flexibility.

When disruptive incidents occur, they rarely turn out exactly as we imagined when planning for them, and overly restrictive procedures can compound problems in the heat of the moment – if, for example, circumstances dictate that the procedure is deployed in a different sequence than planned for. As a result, it is sensible to allow for some degree of flexibility in your response procedures.

Disruptive incidents may also affect communications and, especially in the initial stages, are usually accompanied by no small amount of stress and confusion. Keeping procedures clear and concise goes a long way to ensuring a smooth recovery.

Response structure

This refers to the team (or teams) that direct, lead and implement the response and recovery actions. A common term for the top-level team is the 'crisis management team' (CMT). The CMT should comprise the most appropriate people to make decisions about response actions and to ensure they are implemented in the most effective way.

Every organisation is unique, so there can be no 'standard' CMT, but it should include personnel from all major areas of the organisation to provide the widest possible range of experience and knowledge should an incident occur. Each member of the CMT should be able to understand and assess the impact of a disruption on their respective area of expertise and select appropriate response actions.

Regardless of the make-up of the CMT, it is necessary to define specific responsibilities for each team member, and to designate an 'alternate' for each role in case the primary team member is unavailable.

Warning and communication

You will need to develop procedures for communicating with and responding to interested parties about disruptive incidents and the actions you take to recover from them. These should link to, but are distinct from, the communications procedures for the BCMS (described in section 7 of the Standard) – this requirement is concerned with documenting and coordinating your communication with authorities and other relevant parties during and after an incident, including any necessary media response.

Incident communication procedures should account for the need to communicate with emergency responders and any national risk advisory or alert systems. Perhaps most importantly, the Standard also requires that you develop a procedure that ensures that your means of communication remain available during disruptive incidents. Even the best-laid communication plans will fail if you cannot communicate at all.

Business continuity plans

When developing continuity plans, do not try to develop one plan that accounts for all possible scenarios. Such a plan will be unwieldy, needlessly complex and prone to failure. Instead, develop multiple broad plans for scenarios for which responses are likely to be similar. You might, for example, develop plans for:

- Major site or premises incidents (fires, floods, etc.);
- Information and communications system failures;
- Supply chain failures; and
- Pandemics and similar scenarios.

Approaching continuity plans in this manner allows the CMT to focus on responses to those scenarios, saving time and eliminating unnecessary activity.

Plans should be clear and specific, and directly refer to the predefined thresholds for activating the plan. They should also set out when the plans can be deactivated, how reporting is conducted, the roles and responsibilities of people involved in deploying the plan, the processes that must be used, and any supporting information necessary.

The BCPs should be accessible to all those who will need to use them when activated, so distribution and control of the set of documents that comprise the plan are important elements of the BCMS. Just as the BCP is pivotal, having the wrong version of it when needed could be disastrous.

Although not directly mentioned in this part of the Standard, you should also keep an incident log to support proper accountability and to inform the review and improvement of the BCP and BCMS.

Exercise programme

It is not enough to develop plans and simply assume that they will work when deployed. Many difficulties only reveal themselves in the doing, and the Standard acknowledges this by requiring you to test your plans periodically.

Exercises once or twice a year are typical, the outcome of which should be recorded and evaluated to identify any issues or deficiencies and implement improvements.

Evaluation of business continuity documentation and capabilities

This part of the Standard requires you to evaluate and improve your documentation and recovery capabilities, and should not be confused with the following section, which focuses on evaluating and improving the BCMS itself.

The plans themselves and the documentation they rely on, including the BIA, risk assessments, procedures, measures to ensure legal compliance, etc., should all be reviewed periodically, whether the plans are used or not. They should also be reviewed after any activation of the plan, and after any significant changes to the organisation and how it operates.

You will also need to measure the aspects of the plan and its supporting documentation, etc. that you deem useful to drive improvement. These will differ from organisation to organisation, but might include supplier and contingency response times, whether RTOs are met, whether backups are restored in the expected time frames, whether all stages of a given response procedure are followed, and so on.

9 Performance evaluation

All management systems incorporate performance evaluation to drive improvement. This is achieved through a combination of the following:

- Monitoring, measurement, analysis and evaluation.
- Internal audit.
- Management review.

ISO 22301 leaves it to the organisation to determine what to monitor and how measurement and evaluation are conducted. This leaves many organisations wondering if they're 'doing it right'.

You don't need to monitor or measure every single aspect of your BCMS. You do, however, need to focus on metrics that provide useful information that you can apply to improve it. In practice, this usually means defining key performance indicators (KPIs) for the BCMS, such as total recovery time during exercises, the frequency at which risk assessments are reviewed and updated, or performance against BCMS objectives. Keeping the number of KPIs low (e.g. five or less) helps keep things manageable and focused.

It's not enough just to gather the numbers, either – you need to evaluate and analyse them (and keep some documentation as proof). The output of your analysis drives improvement action, so if the trend in total recovery time during exercises shows that recovery time is increasing, then you can investigate the root cause and take mitigating action.

Audits are another common feature of management systems and are the means by which the organisation ensures that the BCMS conforms to the requirements of the Standard (and any requirements defined by the organisation).

You will need to develop an audit programme that covers all aspects of the BCMS. You will also need to appoint auditors and ensure they are trained to an appropriate standard.[7] The audits themselves should be relatively limited in scope (e.g. is the risk assessment process being followed and are risk assessments updated when they should be?), and should follow any nonconformities to the root cause – this is critical to prevent recurrence. Nonconformities are documented and fed into the corrective action procedure to ensure they are resolved.

The final component of performance evaluation is another factor common to all management systems – the management review. This should occur periodically (e.g. once or twice a year) and is intended to provide top management with a detailed overview of the BCMS. It must include the items noted in the Standard, such as trends in monitoring and measurement results, performance against BCMS objectives, changes to the organisation that might affect the BCMS, risks and opportunities, and so on.

The review must also output the items required by the Standard, though from a practical perspective, most of the necessary outputs will be generated automatically provided the inputs are properly accounted for. The review and its inputs and outputs should be recorded so that you can monitor the evolution of the BCMS and make improvements, and so that you can refer to them in future reviews when evaluating progress.

The management review is a mandatory part of surveillance audits conducted by certification bodies (i.e. it will be checked at every visit by a third-party auditor), so it is important to ensure that every requirement is accounted for.

10 Improvement

The output of your performance evaluation methods feed directly into improvement of the BCMS in two ways:

- Nonconformity and corrective action.

---

[7] For example, the Certified ISO 22301 BCMS Lead Auditor Training Course available from IT Governance, *www.itgovernance.co.uk/shop/product/certified-iso-22301-bcms-lead-auditor-training-course*.

- Continual improvement.

Nonconformity and corrective action

Your audit programme will highlight nonconformities in the BCMS and should also identify the root cause. The findings of the audit report are linked to a corrective action (which must be documented) that lists the nonconformity, the root cause and the proposed solution. The solution is applied and reviewed at a later date to ensure it is effective.

It is important to note that few, if any, management systems remain 'perfect' over time – nonconformities are to be expected as the organisation and the management system evolve. Nonconformities should generally be viewed as an opportunity to improve the BCMS rather than as something negative; however, recurring nonconformities are an indicator that the root cause of the problem is not being properly addressed, and warrant further investigation.

It is common practice to assign nonconformities to one of three categories that describe the severity of the issue: 'major', 'minor' and 'opportunity for improvement'.

1. **Major** – these nonconformities generally refer to the complete absence of a requirement (e.g. no document control system, or no communications procedure), or to prolonged or wilful failure to meet a requirement.
2. **Minor** – these nonconformities generally refer to requirements that are met in part but suffer from some non-critical deficiency (e.g. document control exists but does not provide for version control on some document types, or a work instruction exists but was not used).
3. **Opportunity for improvement** – generally indicates a situation that is acceptable now, but that could result in a problem in the future, such as a leaky roof in a storage area. You can put a bucket underneath the leak for now,

but you should get the roof repaired soon, before the next heavy rainstorm, or risk damage to stored items.

Continual improvement

'Continual improvement' simply means that you must always be looking for ways to improve the BCMS. You will achieve this as a matter of course, provided that your audits and corrective actions, measurement and analysis, management review, etc. are effective, and there is good communication between your crisis management team, top management and the rest of the organisation that allows issues to be raised and corrected.

CHAPTER 6: CERTIFICATION

As with many other management system standards, there is a scheme that organisations can use to demonstrate their compliance with ISO 22301.

In the UK, accredited certification schemes are managed by the United Kingdom Accreditation Service (UKAS) and it would generally be unwise to secure certification from a 'certification body' that is not accredited by UKAS or by another national accreditation body.

Certification is usually a two-stage process involving independent audits conducted by the external certification body.

The initial audit focuses on whether you are implementing the BCMS correctly and in line with the Standard, and will examine various key requirements to ensure they are being met. Don't worry if the auditor discovers nonconformities at this stage – this is normal, and the auditor will use them as an opportunity to help you better understand the requirements of the Standard and how they should be applied.

After the first audit, you will have a clear idea of where you are meeting requirements and where you are falling short. You can then develop an action plan to implement any necessary changes to the fledgling BCMS in preparation for the certification audit.

The certification audit follows a similar process to the first, in that it will examine the various constituent parts of the BCMS to ensure they comply with the Standard. The auditor will look for evidence that the BCMS is implemented, functional and operating effectively, which will likely involve reviewing evidence of audits, measurement analysis, management review, progress against objectives, etc.

The goal should be to begin the certification audit with confidence that there are no major nonconformities in the BCMS. Any minor issues noted can usually be resolved through your corrective action procedures, but any major nonconformities identified will likely result in a further visit from the auditor, with a consequential delay in achieving your certification.

FURTHER READING

IT Governance Publishing (ITGP) is the world's leading publisher for governance and compliance. Our industry-leading pocket guides, books, training resources and toolkits are written by real-world practitioners and thought leaders. They are used globally by audiences of all levels, from students to C-suite executives.

Our high-quality publications cover all IT governance, risk and compliance frameworks and are available in a range of formats. This ensures our customers can access the information they need in the way they need it.

Our other publications about business continuity and ISO 22301 include:

- *Business Continuity and the Pandemic Threat – Potentially the biggest survival challenge facing organisations* by Robert Clark, *www.itgovernancepublishing.co.uk/product/business-continuity-and-the-pandemic-threat*
- *Validating Your Business Continuity Plan – Ensuring your BCP actually works* by Robert Clark, *www.itgovernancepublishing.co.uk/product/validating-your-business-continuity-plan*
- *Disaster Recovery and Business Continuity - A quick guide for organisations and business managers* by Thejendra B.S, *www.itgovernancepublishing.co.uk/product/disaster-recovery-and-business-continuity*

For more information on ITGP and branded publishing services, and to view our full list of publications, visit *www.itgovernancepublishing.co.uk*.

To receive regular updates from ITGP, including information on new publications in your area(s) of interest, sign up for our newsletter *www.itgovernancepublishing.co.uk/topic/newsletter*.

Branded publishing

Through our branded publishing service, you can customise ITGP publications with your company's branding.

Find out more at
www.itgovernancepublishing.co.uk/topic/branded-publishing-services.

Related services

ITGP is part of GRC International Group, which offers a comprehensive range of complementary products and services to help organisations meet their objectives.

For a full range of resources on business continuity and ISO 22301 visit *www.itgovernance.co.uk/shop/category/bcm-and-iso-22301*.

Training services

The IT Governance training programme is built on our extensive practical experience designing and implementing management systems based on ISO standards, best practice and regulations.

Our courses help attendees develop practical skills and comply with contractual and regulatory requirements. They also support career development via recognised qualifications.

Learn more about our training courses in business continuity and ISO 22301 and view the full course catalogue at *www.itgovernance.co.uk/training*.

Professional services and consultancy

We are a leading global consultancy of IT governance, risk management and compliance solutions. We advise businesses around the world on their most critical issues and present cost-saving and risk-reducing solutions based on international best practice and frameworks.

We offer a wide range of delivery methods to suit all budgets, timescales and preferred project approaches.

Find out how our consultancy services can help your organisation at *www.itgovernance.co.uk/consulting*.

Industry news

Want to stay up to date with the latest developments and resources in the IT governance and compliance market? Subscribe to our Weekly Round-up newsletter and we will send you mobile-friendly emails with fresh news and features about your preferred areas of interest, as well as unmissable offers and free resources to help you successfully start your projects. *www.itgovernance.co.uk/weekly-round-up*.

EU for product safety is Stephen Evans, The Mill Enterprise Hub, Stagreenan, Drogheda, Co. Louth, A92 CD3D, Ireland. (servicecentre@itgovernance.eu)

www.ingramcontent.com/pod-product-compliance
Lightning Source LLC
Chambersburg PA
CBHW070904070326
40690CB00009B/1987